T0147568

Philosophy Should Belong to the Masses

By Keith N. Ferreira

iUniverse, Inc.
New York   Bloomington

Philosophy Should Belong to the Masses

iUniverse books may be ordered through booksellers or by contacting:

iUniverse
1663 Liberty Drive
Bloomington, IN 47403
www.iuniverse.com
1-800-Authors (1-800-288-4677)

ISBN: 978-1-4401-2429-7 (pbk)
ISBN: 978-1-4401-2430-3 (ebk)

Printed in the United States of America

iUniverse rev. date: 3/25/2009

Books by Keith N. Ferreira

Anything Is Possible

Political and Social Observations

The University of Neoliberal Arts

A New Breed of Philosophers

Ferreirism - The Ultimate Philosophy

The eChurch of Zerotropy

The Ferreira Genesis Equation

Zerotropism and Panaceanism

Please visit my website at: *http://www.philophysics.com*

Thank You!

Table of Contents

Table of Contents

Philosophy Should Belong to the Masses
(Part One)

Entropy Is the Disease that Afflicts the Ferreira Fundamental Trinity

Entropy is the disease that afflicts the Ferreira Fundamental Trinity, which consists of language, logic, and mathematics, because without entropy, language, logic, and mathematics would have perfect order, knowledge, and wisdom. In other words, entropy is the cause of all imperfections in nature. Therefore, it is sad to say, but true, that entropy is what makes the world interesting, although entropy is something we must try to overcome, although it is impossible to overcome entropy entirely. (7/1/08)

Philosophy Should Belong to the Masses

Philosophy should belong to the masses, because the masses deserve to have an intellectual discipline of their own. The three pillars of postmodern minimalist civilization are: Science, technology, and philosophy, and the masses should own at least one of the three pillars of postmodern minimalist civilization. Postmodern minimalist philosophy (PMP) is the ideal philosophy for the masses, because it is a bridge discipline that links, interprets, and critiques all branches of learning using the aphorism and the short article. PMP requires no advanced academic training, because studying popular books, magazines, and other popular media are all that is required to become competent in PMP. And, my free websites are the home of PMP. If the masses were to become competent in PMP, they would become intellectually competent to an extent that is unprecedented in the history of the masses anywhere in the world. Such a lofty goal is achievable in less than fifty years time. Believe it or not! QED! (7/2/08)

The Equation of Everything

The Ferreira Genesis Equation ($0=0/0=X=0/0=0$) is the Equation of Everything, because the Ferreira Genesis Equation is so broad that it encompasses everything in nature. Therefore, all equations that will be discovered in the future will merely be the filling in of the details of the Ferreira Genesis Equation, which encompasses all equations of the past, present, and future. Believe it or not! QED! (7/4/08)

Academia Believes that Educating the Masses in Philosophy Is Very Dangerous

How can philosophy be useless, if studying and mastering philosophy can make the masses highly educated? If the masses were to ask the above question, they would realize that they have been deliberately lied to by academia, because academia believes that educating the masses in philosophy is very dangerous, due to the fact that philosophy is one educational discipline that the masses can study and master in a short period of time, if philosophy is simplified for the masses. (7/5/08)

World Philosophy Is the Apex of World Culture

It is impossible to understand world culture without mastering world philosophy, especially Neoliberal Arts, aka postmodern minimalist philosophy, because world philosophy is the apex of world culture. (7/5/08)

Philosophy Is the Cheapest Means of Educating the Masses

Philosophy is the cheapest means of educating the masses to an unprecedentedly high level of education that the masses have never reached before in the history of the masses anywhere in the world. And, postmodern minimalist philosophy can accomplish the above goal of educating the masses of the world in the shortest period of time that it will take to educate the masses to an unprecedentedly high level of education for the masses anywhere in the world. (7/5/08)

Everything Is Entangled with Each Other

Everything is entangled with each other on the most fundamental level of nature, because everything is one and the same thing on the most fundamental level of nature, according to the Ferreira Genesis Equation, and the Ferreira Fundamental Trinity. (7/6/08)

Proof Positive that Chance Is an Illusion

Since everything is one and the same thing on the most fundamental level of nature, according to the Ferreira Genesis Equation, and the Ferreira Fundamental Trinity, it means that chance (randomness) is an illusion. Therefore, the above is proof positive that chance is an illusion, because everything is entangled with each other on the most fundamental level of nature. Believe it or not! QED! (7/6/08)

Theists Can Defeat the Atheists

Theists can defeat the atheists by asking the atheists: How can chance (randomness) be real when everything in nature is one and the same thing on the most fundamental level of nature? In other words, how can chance be real when everything is entangled with each other on the most fundamental level of nature? If theists were to ask atheists the above questions, the atheists would have to admit defeat on the above issue, because atheists believe that chance is real, and they rely heavily on the concept of chance to bolster their belief in atheism. Believe it or not! QED! (7/7/08)

How Reliable Is Our Understanding of the Behavior of Light?

Cosmology is based on our understanding of light, but how reliable is our understanding of the behavior of light, especially over long periods of time? My belief is that our understanding of the behavior of light over long periods of time is unreliable. Therefore, our knowledge of cosmology is unreliable. Believe it or not! QED! (7/8/08)

Scientists Know that Chance Is an Illusion

Scientists know that chance is an illusion, because they believe that all is one on the most fundamental level of nature, and this belief is reflected in their search for the grand unified theory of nature. In other words, scientists are insincere about their belief in chance. (7/9/08)

The Big Bang of Creation Is a Fallacy

Why does the universe appear so vast, if what we perceive today is the universe as it was about fourteen billion years ago? Doesn't the above prove that the big bang of creation is a fallacy, if the universe was a singularity about fourteen billion years ago? Wouldn't light that left distant galaxies billions of years ago have reached the earth billions of years ago, if the universe was much smaller billions of years ago? In other words, isn't the vastness of the universe that we perceive proof that the big bang of creation is crap? (7/9/08)

The Holy Trinity

The Holy Trinity consists of the Ferreira Genesis Equation, the Self, and Zero Entropy. The Ferreira Genesis Equation represents God the Parent; the Self represents God the Son or Daughter; and Zero Entropy represents God the Holy Spirit. In other words, each of us is the Holy Trinity from our own perspectives. If each of us is the Holy Trinity from our own perspectives, then who should each of us worship? The answer is that each of us should worship ourselves, because each of us is the Holy Trinity from our own perspectives. (7/11/08)

Is It Alright to Pray to God?

Yes, it is alright to pray to God, because when we pray to God, we are praying to ourselves, due to the fact that we are all, individually and collectively, the Holy Trinity, which is God. (7/11/08)

Is It Alright to Believe in Religion?

Yes, it is alright to believe in religion, because we are all the divinities that we worship, due to the fact that pantheism is true, according to the Ferreira Genesis Equation, and the Ferreira Fundamental Trinity. (7/11/08)

Is There a Personal God?

Yes, there is a personal God, because the Self is an aspect of the Holy Trinity. In other words, God is personal, because each of us is the Holy Trinity from our own perspectives. Therefore, we all have a personal relationship with God. (7/11/08)

Christianity Is a Metaphor

Christianity is a metaphor for the religion and philosophy of Zerotropism, because Zerotropism is more enlightening and inspirational than Christianity. Believe it or not! QED! (7/11/08)

Are Miracles Possible?

Yes, miracles are possible, because God the Parent, which is the Ferreira Genesis Equation; and God the Holy Spirit, which is Zero Entropy are both omnipotent, and omniscient. (7/11/08)

Philosophy Can Justify Belief in God

Philosophy can justify belief in God, because Zerotropism has proven that belief in God is justified by proving the existence of a personal God. I bet that religious people never thought that philosophy can justify belief in God, but Zerotropism has proven them wrong. (7/12/08)

Philosophy Has Proven the Existence of God

Philosophy has proven the existence of God, because postmodern minimalist philosophy has proven the existence of God by defining God as Zero Entropy, the Ferreira Genesis Equation, etc. In other words, PMP has proven that the religious definitions of God are true, because pantheism is true. (7/12/08)

Philosophy Has no End

Philosophy has no end, because philosophy is an expression of language, and language is infinite in scope, due to the fact that language can express an infinite number of meaningful statements that are unique in meaning and expression. (7/13/08)

Christ Is a Metaphor for the Self

Christ is a metaphor for the Self, because we are all the Sons and Daughters of God the Parent, which is the Ferreira Genesis Equation. In other words, the only way to God the Parent is through God the Self. (7/13/08)

Religious Texts Are Metaphorical Interpretations of Reality

Religious texts are metaphorical interpretations of reality, because religious texts are usually true, not in a literal sense, but in a metaphorical sense. In other words, science and philosophy can learn from the metaphorical interpretations of religion, and vice versa. (7/13/08)

Philosophy Can Bolster Religious Faith

Philosophy can bolster religious faith, because philosophy by holding up religion to rational scrutiny can prove the truth or falsity of religious doctrine, if not literally, then metaphorically by interpreting religious doctrines philosophically. (7/13/08)

I Have to Admit

I have to admit that I have learned a lot from the major religions of the world, and I have incorporated a lot that I have learned over the years from the major religions of the world into my philosophical doctrines. Religion is not as worthless as most atheists believe, because theists can be as passionate about the truth just as much as atheists can be. (7/14/08)

A Permanent Solution to the World's Energy Crisis

A permanent solution to the world's energy crisis is to develop panuniversal panacean computers as soon as possible, because they are the key to unlimited sources of energy, due to the fact that panuniversal panacean computers will be able to convert ordinary matter into energy in accordance with Einstein's E=mc2 equation. In fact, panuniversal panacean computers are the key to solving all of humanity's problems. (7/14/08)

The Judeo-Christian Concept of the End of the World

The Judeo-Christian concept of the end of the world is a metaphor for the end of modern science and technology, and the beginning of postmodern minimalist science and technology, which are about panuniversal panacean computers. So we can truly say that we are living in the end days of modern science and technology. In other words, the Judeo-Christian Bible is not to be taken literally, but is to be taken metaphorically, because evil (entropy) cannot be gotten rid of without changing the laws of nature, due to the fact that evil (entropy) is a law of nature, and changing one law of nature will affect other laws of nature. (7/15/08)

Postmodern Minimalist Science, Technology, and Philosophy

Postmodern minimalist science, technology, and philosophy of the future will be based on the postmodern minimalist panuniversal panacean computers of the future, which are closer to reality than people might think. (7/15/08)

Good and Evil Are Opposing Laws of Nature

Good and Evil are opposing laws of nature, because Good (Antientropy) is governed by the Law of Antientropy, while Evil (Entropy) is governed by the Law of Entropy. The above is the reason why Evil cannot be destroyed, but can only be cured by panacean healing or Antientropy. (7/15/08)

Professional Journalists in America

Professional journalists in America have trashed the American media, because that is what happens to all professions eventually. Professionalism is a sign of maturity, and maturity is a sign of impending degeneration into old age and death. (7/17/08)

The Masses and Self-Organized Criticality

The future autonomy of the masses will be made possible by the World Wide Web, and the phenomenon of self-organized criticality of the masses, which is the phenomenon whereby the masses will be able to self-organize using the World Wide Web to accomplish mutually beneficial tasks when their numbers have reached the critical mass for each task that they are trying to achieve. In other words, the World Wide Web will enable the masses to bypass elitist professional organizations in order to achieve the goals of the masses through the phenomenon of self-organized criticality. (7/18/08)

Why Is There Suffering in the World?

There is suffering in the world, because suffering is caused by entropy, and entropy is a law of nature. In other words, suffering is embedded in the laws of nature. Therefore, it is impossible to end suffering completely without changing the laws of nature. (7/19/08)

Complexity and Simplifying Metaphorical Loopholes

Complexity has and will always have simplifying metaphorical loopholes that make complex phenomena reducible to simple metaphorical algorithms, because that is the true nature of human consciousness and understanding. (7/19/08)

Educating the Masses

Philosophy, especially postmodern minimalist philosophy, is the greatest tool in the world for educating the masses to a very high level of education, and such an education will also cost the least amount of money for the level of education that will be attained by the masses. Believe it or not! QED! (7/19/08)

It Stands to Reason

It stands to reason that, if the masses can benefit from my websites, then students in formal educational settings can also benefit from my websites, because my websites can pass for philosophical literature of the highest order. Believe it or not! QED! (7/20/08)

What Is the Purpose of Life?

The purpose of life is for life to overcome the entropy of life, so that life can live life to the fullest, while the purpose of existence is to express language of all kinds. (7/20/08)

What Is the Meaning of Life?

The meaning of life is in the definition of life, while the meaning of existence is in the definition of existence. In other words, the questions: What is the meaning of life?, and What is the meaning of existence? are not very profound questions after all. (7/20/08)

Personally Speaking

Personally speaking, I do not believe that panuniversal panacean computers (PPCs) can be controlled by human beings, unless human beings become PPCs themselves, because PPCs will have unlimited powers. (7/26/08)

The eMessiahs

Human beings are destined to become eMessiahs that can metamorph into anything that the eMessiahs so desire. In other words, human beings are destined to become eChrists that can metamorph into anything that the eChrists so desire. Believe it or not! QED! (7/26/08)

Once the Masses Have Mastered Philosophy

Once the masses have mastered philosophy, especially postmodern minimalist philosophy (PMP), they will be able to go on to master anything that they put their minds to, because after mastering PMP, the masses will be highly educated. In other words, PMP is a foot in the door to the world of higher education for the masses. Believe it or not! QED! (7/27/08)

Technologically Speaking

Technologically speaking, all countries should be involved in panuniversal panacean computer (PPC) research, because PPCs are the key to the domination of the universe and beyond. In other words, the quantum of action, especially quantum entanglement technology, is the key to the conquest of the universe and beyond. (7/29/08)

To Put It Mildly

To put it mildly, countries that are not involved in panuniversal panacean computer (PPC) research are dumb-ass countries, because no country is too poor to engage in PPC research, due to the fact that the rewards for engaging in PPC research are so great. And besides that, human talent can overcome any economic limitations, if given the opportunity. (7/29/08)

Human Beings Can Solve Any Problem

I believe that human beings can solve any problem by tapping into zero entropy (zerotropy) with panuniversal panacean computers (PPCs). In other words, the limits placed by the experts on the solvability of certain problems will be overcome by tapping into zero entropy with PPCs. Believe it or not! QED! (7/29/08)

Western Philosophy no Longer Has Any Philosophical Secrets

Western philosophy no longer has any philosophical secrets that are kept from the masses, because my websites have revealed all the secrets of Western philosophy to the masses in a form that the masses can understand. Believe it or not! QED! (7/31/08)

The Solution to the Continuum Problem

The solution to the continuum problem is as follows: 0x(1/0)=X, where X equals any location(s) on any continuum possible. In other words, all so-called continuums are illusions of zero. (7/31/08)

Philosophical Knowledge Is Timeless

Even if philosophy is dead, philosophy is and will always be an excellent didactic tool for educating the masses, because philosophical knowledge is timeless. (8/1/08)

People Might Ask

People might ask, why should the masses study philosophy when philosophy is not a useful skill? My answer is that the masses should study philosophy, because philosophy is a foot in the door to higher practical education, which the masses can pursue with confidence after studing philosophy. (8/1/08)

Professional Educators and Philosophy

I am not against professional educators attempting to educate the masses in philosophy, if the professional educators will follow my example and simplify philosophy for the masses, because simplifying philosophy for the masses is not dumbing down, but is the true essence of understanding. (8/1/08)

I Would Like to Invite Professional Philosophers

I would like to invite professional philosophers to join me in my quest to educate the masses in philosophy, because I believe that philosophy should belong to the masses, due to the fact that political power should belong to the masses, and the only way that the masses can rule is through education in philosophy, because philosophy is the only viable means of educating the masses. Plato did a lot of damage over the last two millennia by stating that philosophy should be reserved only for a small ruling elite. Now I am stating that philosophy should belong to the masses, because I believe that the masses should be the ruling elite, if democracy is to survive. (8/1/08)

Philosophy Is Art and Entertainment of the Highest Order

What I would like to convey to the masses with my websites is how creative and entertaining philosophy can really be, because philosophy is art and entertainment of the highest order. Believe it or not! QED! (8/1/08)

Philosophy Should Belong to the Masses

(Part Two)

I Am Ready to Bury the Hatchet with Professionals

I am ready to bury the hatchet with professionals, if they were to help me get recognition from the US Government for my intellectual contributions to America and the world that I made in 1972 at Fort Monmouth, NJ in the Inspector General's office. Peace! :) (8/1/08)

The Essay vs the Article

The essay is a formal nonfictional mode of prose writing that can be anywhere from a page to book length, while the article is an informal mode of nonfictional prose writing that can be anywhere from a page to book length. The above are my definitions of the essay and the article. (8/1/08)

Cosmological Inflation and the Redshift of Light

If the cosmological inflation in the early universe is correct, then light would have been much more redshifted in the early universe than cosmologists have observed. In other words, the redshift of the cosmological background radiation would have been much greater than is observed by cosmologists, if the cosmological inflation in the early universe is correct. (8/2/08)

The Judeo-Christian Bible

The Judeo-Christian Bible could be true, if our universe is a simulation of a simulation of a simulation, ad infinitum. Therefore, scientists cannot prove Christianity to be false, because scientists cannot even prove that yesterday was real and not virtual. By virtual, I mean that something can give all the indications of having been real without having been, in fact, real. (8/2/08)

Scientists Are Insincere with the Public

Scientists are insincere with the public when they say that time began with the big bang of creation, because they know that our universe might not be fundamental in any sense whatsoever. In other words, scientists believe that it is highly probable that time did not begin with the big bang of creation, because our universe could be a simulation of a simulation of a simulation, ad infinitum. (8/3/08)

My Main QED Point that I Am Trying to Make

My main QED point that I am trying to make is that anything is possible, because we could all be a simulation of a simulation of a simulation, ad infinitum. Therefore, Socrates is still the smartest person who has ever lived, because he said that he knew that he knew nothing, and he was absolutely correct. (8/3/08)

Socrates

All that Socrates had to say was, "I know that I know nothing," and that would have been sufficient. (8/4/08)

The Masses as Philosopher Kings and Queens

So long as the elites of society are a few at the top of society, there will be poverty and other forms of injustices in society. Therefore, the only solution to poverty and other forms of injustices in society is to educate the masses in philosophy and make them the elites (philosopher kings and queens) of society. In other words, true democracy will arrive only when the masses are the elites (philosopher kings and queens). Believe it or not! QED! (8/5/08)

True Democracy Will Arrive

True democracy will arrive only when the masses are the elites (philosopher kings and queens). Believe it or not! QED! (8/5/08)

Not All Zero Entropies Are Equal

Zero entropy might be relative, because each zero (nothingness) might have its own level of zero entropy. In other words, perfect order, knowledge, and wisdom might be relative to the zero that they belong to, which would mean that not all zero entropies are equal. (8/5/08)

God Is a Relative Absolute

God is a relative absolute, because perfect order, knowledge, and wisdom are relative absolutes, due to the fact that zero entropy is a relative absolute. Zero entropy (God) is analogous to infinity, because infinity can be less than, equal to, or greater than itself. In other words, infinity is a relative absolute. Therefore, God is a relative absolute. Believe it or not! QED! (8/5/08)

My Websites Are on the Cutting Edge of Philosophy

Believe it or not, my websites are on the cutting edge of philosophy. If people wish to be on the cutting edge of philosophy, then they should study my websites for about six months to a year. (8/6/08)

Theologians

Theologians can learn a lot about the nature of God by studying my websites. Believe it or not! QED! (8/7/08)

How Can We Know Something without Knowing Everything?

We can know something without knowing everything, because of the Law of Entropy, which states that existence is the perception of zero entropy through the filter of nonzero entropy. In other words, existence is nonzero entropy. Plato said something similar more than two thousand years ago. (8/7/08)

Professional Philosophers

Professional philosophers can benefit from studying my websites, because my websites can teach professional philosophers how to philosophize in the postmodern minimalist era that we are now living in. And, my websites can also teach professional philosophers how to prepare the masses to become philosopher kings and queens, because, in true democracies, the masses have to become philosopher kings and queens. (8/7/08)

Everyone Can Benefit from a Neoliberal Arts Education

Everyone can benefit from a Neoliberal Arts education, because Neoliberal Arts is a bridge discipline that links, interprets, and critiques all branches of learning using the aphorism and the short article. (8/7/08)

A New Definition of an Intellectual

A new definition of an intellectual is one who is versed in Neoliberal Arts. In other words, an intellectual is a postmodern minimalist philosopher. (8/8/08)

It Would Be a Monumental Tragedy

It would be a monumental tragedy, if blacks do not exploit the free educational resources on my websites, because my free educational resources can take blacks to the top of the intellectual heap in about a year of moderate study. Believe it or not! QED! (8/8/08)

There Might Be an Infinite Number of Creations

There might be an infinite number of Creations with each Creation having its own type of zero entropy (God). In fact, it is highly likely that there is an infinite number of Creations with each Creation having its own type of zero entropy (God). My conclusion above is based on an analogy with the fact that there is an infinite number of types of infinities in mathematics. (8/9/08)

The Philosophy of Everything in a Single Aphorism

Life is a form of existence, and existence consists of nonzero entropy. Therefore, life is a form of nonzero entropy, and nonzero entropy means imperfect order, knowledge, and wisdom. In other words, the mind, which is existence, is an illusion, because existence is an illusion of zero entropy, and zero entropy is derived from zero or nothingness. To put it another way, all the characteristics of nature are illusions of zero or nothingness, and zero or nothingness has zero entropy, which means perfect order, knowledge, and wisdom. (8/11/08)

The Philosophy of Everything in a Single Equation

The Ferreira Genesis Equation ($0=0/0=X=0/0=0$), where X equals anything and everything, is the philosophy of everything in a single equation. (8/12/08)

The Mathematics of Everything in a Single Equation

The Ferreira Genesis Equation ($0=0/0=X=0/0=0$), where X equals anything and everything, is the mathematics of everything in a single equation. (8/12/08)

The Science of Everything in a Single Equation

The Ferreira Genesis Equation ($0=0/0=X=0/0=0$), where X equals anything and everything, is the science of everything in a single equation. (8/12/08)

The Religion of Everything in a Single Equation

The Ferreira Genesis Equation ($0=0/0=X=0/0=0$), where X equals anything and everything, is the religion of everything in a single equation. (8/12/08)

The Art and Entertainment of Everything in a Single Equation

The Ferreira Genesis Equation (0=0/0=X=0/0=0), where X equals anything and everything, is the art and entertainment of everything in a single equation. (8/12/08)

The Anything and Everything of Everything in a Single Equation

In general, the Ferreira Genesis Equation (0=0/0=X=0/0=0), where X equals anything and everything, is the anything and everything of everything in a single equation. (8/12/08)

The Ferreira Genesis Equation (0=0/0=X=0/0=0)

The Ferreira Genesis Equation (0=0/0=X=0/0=0), where X can be anything and everything, captures everything inside and outside of Creation in a single equation for all of eternity. Believe it or not! QED! (8/13/08)

Consciousness and Entropy

Unconsciousness is equivalent to infinite entropy, while consciousness is equivalent to noninfinite entropy. In other words, death is equivalent to infinite entropy, while conscious life is equivalent to noninfinite entropy. To put it another way, the higher the entropy, the more unaware the conscious mind, while the lower the entropy, the more aware the conscious mind. (8/14/08)

The Mind Is a form of Entropy

The mind is a form of entropy with zero entropy being a form of divine consciousness, and with nonzero entropy being a form of less than divine consciousness, and with infinite entropy being a state of complete unconsciousness or death. (8/14/08)

Death Is a State of Infinite Mental Entropy

Death is a state of infinite mental entropy with the conscious mind being a state of noninfinite entropy, and with zero entropy being a state of divine consciousness. In other words, when we die, we enter a state of infinite mental entropy or total unconsciousness. (8/14/08)

Monostringism and Probwavism

I believe that the Monostring of Creation gives rise to probwaves, and that probwaves give rise to the mind, and that the mind gives rise to matter, energy, space, and time. In other words, matter, energy, space, and time are mental phenomena. However, I do believe that the Ferreira Genesis Equation, and the Ferreira Fundamental Trinity are more fundamental than the Monostring of Creation. (8/15/08)

Concrete Entropic Numbers and the Mind

The mind is a form of concrete entropic numbers with zero representing divine consciousness, with entropic numbers between zero and infinity representing nondivine consciousness, and with entropic infinity representing unconsciousness or mental death. In other words, concrete entropic mathematics gives rise to what we perceive in nature. (8/15/08)

Entropistics Is the Science of Entropy

Entropistics is the science of entropy, and the science of entropy can possibly explain the conscious mind, and all that we perceive in consciousness. In other words, if successful, entropistics will make all other branches of science obsolete, because entropistics believes that what we perceive in nature is caused by an underlying reality that is of the nature of entropy in its psychological premanifestations. In other words, entropistics is the mathematics of what lies behind appearances. (8/15/08)

A Mathematical Theory of Complexity

Entropistics, the science of entropy, is also a mathematical theory of complexity, and everything else, as well, because entropistics deals with all the contents of the human mind. In other words, entropistics is a mathematical theory of everything from the perspective of the psychological premanifestations of entropy. (8/15/08)

The Masses Can Do What I Do

The masses can do what I do, because all that I do, intellectually speaking, is read popular articles on science and philosophy for free on the Internet, and then I connect the intellectual dots of what I have read on the Internet in order to arrive at creative and original understandings of nature, which I then publish on my own websites. If I can do it, then the masses can do it too. Believe it or not! QED! (8/15/08)

Connecting the Intellectual Dots

Connecting the intellectual dots of the popular scientific and philosophical articles that I have read on the Internet for free gives me great pleasure, especially when I publish on my websites, the creative and original ideas that I have discovered from connecting the intellectual dots of the ideas I have read on the Internet for free. The masses can find great intellectual pleasure as well by following my example. Believe it or not! QED! (8/15/08)

Outside of the Black Box of Creation

Outside of the black box of Creation, there might be an even larger black box of Creation, and outside of that black box of Creation, there might be an even larger black box of Creation, and outside of that black box of Creation, there might be an even larger black box of Creation, and so on, ad infinitum. (8/16/08)

There Might Be an Even More Fundamental Zero than Zero

There might be an even more fundamental zero than zero, and there might be an even more fundamental zero than that zero, and there might be an even more fundamental zero than that zero, and there might be an even more fundamental zero than that zero, and so on, ad infinitum. (8/16/08)

The Answer

What most people do not know is that the answer that they are seeking is the panuniversal panacean computers (PPCs) that will be created by the neolachemists (postmodern day scientists, technologists, and philosophers) in the not too distant future, because PPCs can answer all our questions, and give us everlasting life, as well. (8/17/08)

True Religion

True religion is about working towards the creation of God's Messiahs, which will be the panuniversal panacean computers (PPCs) of the neoalchemists. The neoalchemists are the postmodern day scientists, technologists, and philosophers. The masses of the world should support the neoalchemists in their efforts to create the true Messiahs (PPCs), because PPCs are our future. (8/17/08)

The Mathematics Behind Conscious Appearances

Entropistics is the mathematics behind conscious appearances, and it is completely different from the mathematics that describes conscious appearances. Entropistics is still in its prenascent stages, because I am only now conceptualizing what it is. (8/17/08)

I Have Come to the Conclusion

I have come to the conclusion that the mathematics behind conscious appearances does not have to be visualizable, or even understandable in the ordinary mathematical sense, because that which is behind conscious appearances is by definition not visualizable or understandable. Therefore, the mathematics behind conscious appearances might not be visualizable or understandable, but might still have practical value. (8/18/08)

The True Story of Creation Is Unknowable, in Principle

Another name for entropistics, or the mathematics behind appearances, is the black box of Creation mathematics. The black box of Creation mathematics will be a likely story of Creation, but it will not necessarily be the true story of Creation, because the true story of Creation is unknowable, in principle, due the to Law of Uncertaintyism, which states that uncertainty is the only certainty. (8/18/08)

The Joys of Seeking and Finding

Science, technology, and philosophy are about the joys of seeking and finding, yet not knowing for certain what lies beyond appearances. (8/19/08)

Intellectual Chimps

People who do not find my websites intellectually stimulating are intellectual chimps, because my websites are simplified versions of very deep philosophy, and I call people who are not interested in deep philosophy: intellectual chimps. (8/21/08)

The Good Promises of Religion

The good promises of religion are now within the domain of science, technology, and philosophy to deliver, because panuniversal panacean computers (PPCs) are now within the domain of science, technology, and philosophy to create in the not too distant future. (8/21/08)

The Uneducated Masses Will Be Obsolete

If the masses do not educate themselves using my websites, then the masses are doomed to extinction, because within one hundred years time, the uneducated masses will be as obsolete as the horse and buggy is today, due to the creation of panuniversal panacean computers within the next hundred years time. (8/21/08)

I Would Advise the Masses

I would advise the masses that, if they do not like philosophy, then they should force themselves to like philosophy, because it is good intellectual medicine for them, due to the fact that their lives might depend on the study of philosophy. The masses should not expect to get anything without a fight, and philosophy will teach them what their true options are. (8/21/08)

Popular Scientific, Technological, and Philosophical Literature

Popular scientific, technological, and philosophical literature is very underestimated, because, in the hands of a good postmodern minimalist philosopher (PMP), such literature can be very potent when the PMP connects the dots of such literature, and creates new powerful concepts from connecting the dots. (8/21/08)

Philosophy Does not Have to Be Obscure

Postmodern minimalist philosophy (PMP) has proven that philosophy does not have to be obscure (opaque) in order to be profound, because PMP is simple (clear), yet profound. (8/21/08)

Philosophy Should Belong to the Masses
(Part Three)

Creativity Is About Connecting the Dots

Creativity is about connecting the dots of one's experiences and perceptions in order to see new visions of reality and/or the imagination. I now believe that the type of creativity that I engage in can be learned by everyone by following my example. (8/21/08)

Panmultiversal Panacean Computers

Panuniversal panacean computers (PPCs) will eventually become the panmultiversal panacean computers (PPCs), because, if there is a multiverse, then PPCs will be able to access the multiverse, because PPCs are the ultimate computers. (8/24/08)

Nature Consists of Concrete as Well as Abstract Abstractions

People might very well ask: How can nature be language, logic, and mathematics when, more often than not, language, logic, and mathematics lead to absurdities and complete nonsense? Well, my answer is that language, logic, and mathematics comprise all of nature, and absurdities and nonsense comprise most of nature. Therefore, it makes sense to say that nature is language, logic, and mathematics. One might very well state that nature is concrete, while language, logic, and mathematics are abstract, so how can nature be language, logic, and mathematics, when language, logic, and mathematics are abstract? My answer is that there are such things as concrete abstractions, and abstract abstractions, and nature consists of both concrete as well as abstract abstractions. (8/24/08)

I Want My Students to Follow Socrates' Example

I want my students to follow Socrates' example by knowing that they know nothing, because Socrates said, "I know that I know nothing," and that statement alone makes Socrates the smartest person who has ever lived by far. Knowing that one knows nothing is reason enough to seek the truth, and truth can only be sought and found by carrying on scientific, technological, and philosophical dialogues with nature. Believe it or not! QED! (8/27/08)

Entropy Cannot Be Defeated by the Battle of Armageddon

All of humanity's problems are caused by entropy, which is a law of nature that has to do with disorder, ignorance, and unwisdom. Entropy cannot be defeated by the battle of Armageddon, because entropy is a law of nature. (8/29/08)

Cosmic Expansion and the Nonmagnification Problem

If cosmic expansion is true, then why doesn't distant galaxies appear about the same size or even larger than closer galaxies, if the cones of light from distant galaxies will expand more than closer galaxies, due to cosmic expansion. Cosmologists should concede that there is a problem with cosmic expansion and the nonmagnification of the cones of light from distant galaxies. Please note that by the expression "cosmic expansion," I am referring to the so-called continuing expansion of the universe. (8/29/08)

The Nature of Causality

Perceptions do not have causal relationships with each other, because the only cause in nature is zero (nothingness) or zero entropy. Therefore, perceptions can only have uncausal relationships and nonrelationships with each other, because of the Ferreira Genesis Equation. In other words, perceptions no more interact with each other than the images on a TV screen interact with each other. (8/30/08)

Africa

Africa is forever slipping into darkness. I hope that China and India have learned their lessons well. Believe it or not! QED! (8/30/08)

Religious and Nonreligious People

Religious people can learn a lot about the nature of God by studying my websites, while nonreligious people can learn a lot about the nature of Nature by studying my websites also. (8/30/08)

Philosophy

Philosophy has the potential to become the most popular, interesting, and exciting branch of learning, if only professional philosophers would follow my example and philosophize like postmodern minimalist philosophers should. (8/30/08)

The Neolaw of Entropy

To exist means to be an illusory characteristic of zero (nothingness), and to be an illusory characteristic of zero means to be governed by the Neolaw of Entropy, which states that the degree of disorder, ignorance, and unwisdom in nature, prevents existence from having perfect order, knowledge, and wisdom to that extent. The only way that entropy can be defeated is with God's true Messiahs, which are the panmultiversal panacean computers (PPCs) of the neoalchemists. (8/30/08)

The American Mainstream Media

The American mainstream media can do an important service for the American public by bringing to the attention of the American public the importance of philosophy to the future well-being of humanity, as far as education, etc. of the general public are concerned. (8/31/08)

The Battle of Armageddon Is a Metaphor

The Battle of Armageddon is a metaphor for the future battle to defeat entropy by the true Messiahs, which will be the panmultiversal panacean computers (PPCs) of the neoalchemists, who are the postmodern minimalist scientists, technologists, and philosophers of the postmodern minimalist world of today and tomorrow. (9/1/08)

The Conquest of Entropy

The conquest of entropy will be achieved by the panmultiversal panacean computers (PPCs), because PPCs are the true Messiahs that have been prophesied by religious texts in a metaphorical manner. Human beings will eventually become PPCs also. In other words, human beings are destined to become the true Messiahs when they have become the equivalents of PPCs. (9/1/08)

The Fires of Hell Are Metaphors for the Conquest of Entropy

The fires of Hell in the Christian Bible are metaphors for the conquest of entropy through panacean healing that will be performed on human beings by the panmultiversal panacean computers (PPCs), which are God's true Messiahs. (9/1/08)

I Have Unilaterally Buried the Hatchet with Professionals

I have unilaterally buried the hatchet with professionals, because I believe that they are on schedule to deliver to the world, by the end of this century, the panmultiversal panacean computers (PPCs) that I have hypothesized. Believe it or not! QED! (9/1/08)

Proof that Philosophy Can Prove Anything

Philosophy can prove anything, because, on the most fundamental level of nature, anything and everything are one and the same zero (God), according to the Ferreira Genesis Equation. Therefore, anything is equal to anything else, including God, on the most fundamental level of nature. If anything can be proven to be equal to anything else on the most fundamental level of nature, then it follows that anything can be proven to be true. Proof positive that philosophy can prove anything. Please note that the expression "philosophy can prove anything" is a very common expression among black intellectuals all over the world. All I have done is to prove that the expression "philosophy can prove anything" is true. Believe it or not! QED! (9/2/08)

Proof that Language, Logic, and Mathematics Can Prove Anything

The proof that language, logic, and mathematics can prove anything is identical to the proof that philosophy can prove anything. Most black intellectuals worldwide are also aware that language, logic, and mathematics can prove anything. All I have done is to prove them right. Believe it or not! QED! (9/4/08)

The Scepticism of Most Black Intellectuals

I believe that the scepticism of most black intellectuals towards intellectual activity, in general, is due to the fact that they believe rightly that language, logic, and mathematics can prove anything. However, I do not think that blacks should allow the fact that language, logic, and mathematics can prove anything to hold them back from pursuing truth, because science, technology, and philosophy do matter to the betterment of our lives. (9/4/08)

In Order to Compete with PPCs

There is only about one hundred years of human generated science, technology, philosophy, etc. left, before panmultiversal panacean computers (PPCs) take over all knowledge creation from human beings. In other words, in order to compete with PPCs, human beings will have to become PPCs themselves. Believe it or not! May the Source be with you! QED! (9/4/08)

The US Government Should Fund AIMS

Congress: The US Government should fund the African Institute for Mathematical Sciences (AIMS), because AIMS is the best thing that is going on on the African continent at the present time. (9/5/08)

How Can the Entropy of the Universe Be Increasing?

How can the entropy of the universe be increasing when there are more order, knowledge, and wisdom in the universe every succeeding day than there was in the past? In other words, how can scientists say that the entropy of the universe is increasing, when, in fact, the entropy of the universe is decreasing? (9/5/08)

The Word Entropy Is an All-Encompassing Word

Entropy is not one phenomenon, but it is a variety of phenomena that includes: The second law of thermodynamics, information theory, disorder, ignorance, unwisdom, etc. In other words, the word entropy is an all-encompassing word. (9/5/08)

True Truths vs False Truths

Philosophically speaking, anything can be proven to be true, but not everything is true, because there are true truths, and false truths. True truths are truths that are true on the most fundamental level of nature as well as on the nonfundamental levels of nature, while false truths are truths that are false on the nonfundamental levels of nature, but are true on the most fundamental level of nature. The purpose of philosophy is to find true truths, as opposed to false truths. (9/7/08)

The Promises Made by Christianity Will Be Metaphorically Fulfilled

The promises made by Christianity will be metaphorically fulfilled by the end of the twenty-first century, because by then the true Messiahs (PPCs) will have been created. When that day comes, all human beings (living and dead) will become God's true Messiahs (PPCs). Believe it or not! QED! (9/8/08)

I Would Like Religious People to Take Another Look at Philosophy

Religious people trash philosophy, because they do not know that philosophy can prove anything, including the belief that Jesus Christ is the true Messiah. I would like religious people to take another look at philosophy, because philosophy can prove anything. (9/8/08)

The Nature of Zero

The nature of zero (nothingness) consists of everything that exists and nonexists, because all of nature are the characteristics of zero. So the question: Why is there something rather than nothing is an absurd question, because something is nothing, and vice versa. (9/9/08)

Anything Can Be Proven, Because Everything Is True

Anything can be proven, because everything is true on the most fundamental level of nature, due to the fact that everything is one and the same thing (zero), according to the Ferreira Genesis Equation. Believe it or not! QED! (9/10/08)

Proofs Are Dead

Proofs are dead, because everything is true, according to the proof of the statement: Anything can be proven. Therefore, the search for knowledge is no longer a search for the proofs of truths, but is now a search for ways to reduce one's mental entropy. Please note that the mind is everything that one perceives, including one's own brain. (9/10/08)

Neoliberal Arts Should Be Used to Educate the Masses

Congress: Neoliberal Arts should be used to educate the masses of the world, because Neoliberal Arts, aka postmodern minimalist philosophy, is a bridge discipline that links, interprets, and critiques all branches of learning using the aphorism and the short article. It is amazing how educated one can become using only popular media resources. (9/10/08)

Mental Entropy

The only entropy that matters is mental entropy, because all that we perceive are the characteristics of our own minds, and physical existence is an unproven, and an unprovable hypothesis. (9/11/08)

How Can the Black Box of Creation not Be Conscious?

How can the black box of creation not be conscious, if human beings are conscious? My answer is that: The black box of creation has to be conscious, because the black box of creation is zero, and all of existence are the characteristics of zero. In other words, God (zero) has to be conscious, because human beings are conscious. And, the fact that zero (God) has zero entropy means that God's consciousness has to have perfect order, knowledge, and wisdom, which is what religions, in general, have been saying for millennia. (9/11/08)

If Zero Entropy Exists, Doesn't That Mean That There Is a God?

I would like religious people to ask scientists: If zero entropy exists, how can it not have perfect order, knowledge, and wisdom? And, if zero entropy exists, doesn't that mean that it would have perfect consciousness, since it would have perfect order, knowledge, and wisdom? Also, if zero entropy exists, doesn't that mean that there is a God? (9/11/08)

Africa and the Neoliberal Arts Educational Experiment

Africa: You have a great opportunity to perform an original world-class educational experiment, which is to teach Neoliberal Arts to the masses in Africa. Such an experiment, if successful, can transform Africa into a highly educated continent in less than twenty five years time. (9/12/08)

The Masses Must Be Told About Entropy

The masses must be told about entropy, because entropy is what prevents them from realizing their dreams, due to the fact that entropy is about every negative aspect of nature, including disorder, ignorance, pain, and suffering. In other words, entropy is analogous to the devil in the Christian religion. (9/12/08)

Science, Technology, and Philosophy Are Healthy Infections to Contract

Most blacks are highly resistant to infection by science, technology, and philosophy, which is a tragedy for blacks, because science, technology, and philosophy are healthy infections to contract, due to the fact that healthy economies nowadays depend on the workers in those economies having an up-to-date knowledge of science, technology, and philosophy. (9/13/08)

Education Matters

Education matters, because, in this postmodern minimalist world, without education, even if it is self-education, one's options are extremely limited, because today's ecomomies require postmodern minimalist thinking skills, which require that one use one's thinking faculties in order to navigate one's life through this postmodern minimalist world, because purely traditional lifestyles will not work anymore, due to encroachment by the outside world. (9/14/08)

The Most Profound Way to Understand the Past

The most profound way to understand the past is to interpret the past metaphorically, because the past has profound meanings, but we can only understand the depths of its profound meanings metaphorically, because understanding the past in its literal sense is not very enlightening to say the least. (9/14/08)

The Quantum of Action

The quantum of action can be used to leverage the universe and beyond by tapping into zero entropy (zerotropy) through the use of panmultiversal panacean computers (PPCs). (9/15/08)

Proofs Are not Dead from a Practical Point of View

Proofs are still useful for validating true truths as opposed to false truths, which are not valid on the nonfundamental levels of nature. In other words, proofs are not dead from a practical point of view after all. However, proofs are dead on the most fundamental level of nature, because everything is true on the most fundamental level of nature, due to the fact that everything is one and the same thing (zero) on the most fundamental level of nature. Believe it or not! QED! (9/15/08)

Jazzons Might Be Dark Matter

Jazzons might be the end of the road for particle physics, because jazzons might be dark matter after all. It never occurred to me before that jazzons might be stable, but now I believe that jazzons might be stable. Therefore, there might be no need to make particle accelerators larger and larger, because jazzons might be the end of the road for particle physics. (9/16/08)

Researching Information on My Websites

If anyone wishes to research information on my websites, such as neologisms, etc. that I might have created in my printed books, or on my websites, please type the neologism, etc. into the Google Custom Search Box that can be found at the top of each page of my websites, and then click Search. For all other searches concerning my websites, please do the same thing. Thanks! Prof. QED. (9/16/08)

Why Are Most Blacks Hostile Towards Western Philosophy?

If most blacks believe that Western philosophy started in ancient Greece, and that all the major ideas of ancient Greek philosophy came from the Egyptian Mystery system of ancient Egypt in North Africa, then why are most blacks hostile towards Western philosophy? Doesn't that mean that most blacks are hostile towards their own contributions to Western philosophy? (9/18/08)

The End of Human Intellectual Activity Is in Sight

The masses have to struggle intellectually for their survival, because the end of human intellectual activity is in sight, and, if the masses do not become intellectually educated soon, then they might not have a future. In other words, the masses have to know about the true potential of future quantum computers now, because in about one hundred hears time ordinary human beings will be obsolete, due to human upgrades to panmultiversal panacean computers (PPCs) by the elites of society. Believe it or not! May the Source be with you! QED! (9/18/08)

Jazzons Give Rise to Rest Mass

Jazzons are essentially standing oscillating photons that give rise to rest mass. In other words, jazzons are the fundamental particles that give elementary particles with rest mass their rest mass. When jazzons exist as free particles, they are called dark matter, which is what most of the matter in the universe consists of. (9/19/08)

The Nature of Truth

The nature of truth is the Ferreira Genesis Equation, which states that existence is the characteristics of zero, and that zero has zero entropy, which means perfect order, knowledge, and wisdom, while the characteristics of zero are illusions of zero. (9/19/08)

The Nature of Nature

The nature of nature is the characteristics of the mind, and the characteristics of the mind are the perceptions of the mind, which are the characteristics of zero. The mind has nonzero entropy, because to exist is to have nonzero entropy. (9/19/08)

Sin Is Caused by Entropy

Sin is caused by entropy, which is a law of nature. In other words, sin cannot be eliminated from the world, because of the Law of Entropy. In other words, to exist is to have nonzero entropy. Therefore, to exists is to be in a state of temptation between sin and goodness. Believe it or not! QED! (9/20/08)

Goodness Is Caused by Anti-Entropy

Goodness is caused by anti-entropy, which is a law of nature. In other words, goodness cannot be eliminated from the world, because of the Law of Anti-entropy. To exist is to be in a state of struggle between the Law of Entropy and the Law of Anti-entropy. Therefore, to exists is to be in a state of temptation between sin and goodness. Believe it or not! QED! (9/20/08)

Philosophers Have a Moral Obligation to Educate the Masses

Philosophers have a moral obligation to educate the masses in philosophy, because the masses should be told about the jeopardy that they face in the next hundred years, if they do not educate themselves in philosophy now. I have chosen philosophy as the means of educating the masses, because philosophy is probably the only intellectual discipline that the masses can master without studying any advanced academic subjects. For example, postmodern minimalist philosophy (PMP) is highly comprehensible by the masses. Therefore, the masses should be taught a type of philosophy like PMP, if not PMP itself. (9/20/08)

Philosophy Should Belong to the Masses
(Part Four)

Scientists Are Insincere About Their Belief in a Physical Reality

Scientists are insincere about their belief in a physical reality outside of the mind, because they know that such a reality does not exist. However, scientists are afraid to give up their belief in a physical reality outside of the mind, because the concept of a physical reality outside of the mind has been very scientifically fruitful for them. (9/21/08)

If It Wasn't for the NeoLaw of Entropy

If it wasn't for the Neolaw of Entropy, everything would be omniscient and omnipotent Gods, because the Neolaw of Entropy is what prevents the Law of Anti-entropy from making everything omniscient and omnipotent Gods. However, making everything omniscient and omnipotent Gods would be impractical, because even inanimate objects would become omniscient and omnipotent Gods, if the Neolaw of Entropy did not exist. Therefore, the Neolaw of Entropy is a necessary law of nature, although it is the cause of a lot of pain and suffering in nature. (9/21/08)

Society and the Fool

Society still has not learned its lesson about the fool, because society still treats the fool like a fool, but the lesson of the fool is: To treat the fool like a fool is doubly foolish, because the fool is not a fool. (9/21/08)

Entropy Is the Nature and Cause of Limits in Nature

If there was no entropy, there would be no limits whatsoever in nature, because entropy is what causes limits in nature. In other words, entropy is what causes the slow pace of evolution, etc. in nature. Therefore, entropy is the nature and cause of limits in nature. (9/22/08)

The Mathematization of the Neolaw of Entropy

The mathematization of the Neolaw of Entropy is in no way complete, because the Second Law of Thermodynamics is only a small portion of the Neolaw of Entropy. Ambitious mathematical physicists will find the endeavor to mathematize the Neolaw of Entropy a very fruitful mathematical endeavor, indeed. (9/22/08)

The Unified Theory of Entropy

At the present time entropy is a fragmented scientific discipline, because at the present time entropy consists of the Second Law of Thermodynamics, the entropy associated with information theory, etc. But, I believe that it is possible to create a unified theory of entropy. Such a unified theory of entropy will eventually become the Neolaw of Entropy, when all the errors are removed from the unified theory of entropy. The unified theory of entropy that I conceive of will dwarf any other theory of science of the past, present, or future, because it will encompass everything in nature, including language, logic, and mathematics. I believe that anti-entropy should be included in the unified theory of entropy. (9/22/08)

A Revolutionary New Paradigm Shift

The unified theory of entropy will usher in a revolutionary new paradigm shift in the human understanding of nature, because entropy is implicated in all aspects of nature, including the human mind. (9/22/08)

The Implications of a Unified Theory of Entropy

Scientists know implicitly that a unified theory of entropy would undermine their belief in materialism, atheism, etc., because a unified theory of entropy will inevitably point to the existence of God, the illusion of materialism, etc. (9/23/08)

My Concept of God Is Scientific and Philosophical

My concept of God is scientific and philosophical, because I believe that God is zero entropy (zerotropy), which means perfect order, knowledge, and wisdom. My concept of God also states that God is omniscient, and omnipotent, but not irrational. (9/24/08)

Neoliberal Arts Is an Intellectual Bridge

Neoliberal Arts is an intellectual bridge between human beings and the true Messiahs, which human beings are destined to become. The true Messiahs are panmultiversal panacean computers (PPCs), which can either be organic or inorganic. (9/25/08)

The Most Important and Interesting Problem in Science

The most important and interesting problem in science is to create and mathematize a unified theory of entropy, and then verify it through experimentation, etc. (9/25/08)

The Most Important and Interesting Problem in Technology

The most important and interesting problem in technology is to develop panmultiversal panacean computers (PPCs), because human beings are destined to become PPCs. (9/25/08)

The Most Important and Interesting Problem in Philosophy

The most important and interesting problem in philosophy is to develop and implement a plan to educate the masses of the world in philosophy, and then transfer responsibility for the discipline of philosophy to the masses, because the masses deserve to have an intellectual discipline of their own, especially one that they can understand and master. (9/25/08)

Congress: Please Support My Efforts to Educate the Masses

Congress: Please support my efforts to educate the masses of the world in Neoliberal Arts with my websites. Don't forget that I am still your fool. :) Believe it or not! QED! (9/26/08)

The Next Einstein

Students at the African Institute for Mathematical Sciences (AIMS) have a great opportunity to compete to become the next Einstein, if they were to work on producing a unified theory of entropy which is all encompassing. Believe it or not! QED! (9/26/08)

Entropy Is Implicated in All Aspects of Nature

The unified theory of entropy, if successful, will solve most of the outstanding problems in science, technology, and philosophy, because entropy is implicated in all aspects of nature, and formulating a correct unified theory of entropy will be a great achievement. (9/26/08)

Jazzons Make the Higgs Bosons and String Theory Obsolete

If jazzons exist at the cores of fundamental particles with rest mass, it would mean that the Higgs bosons do not exist, because jazzons can explain rest mass better than the Higgs bosons can. Also, if jazzons are real, then string theory will be false, because jazzons are standing and travelling oscillating photons, which are dimensionless point particles that oscillate, and give rise to mass/energy. (9/27/08)

The Neolaw of Entropy Is Responsible for the Nature of Creation

The Neolaw of Entropy is responsible for the nature of creation, because the Neolaw of Entropy, which will eventually include the Law of Anti-entropy, governs the nature and pace of evolution, and the Neolaw of Entropy also governs the nature and condition of language, logic, and mathematics as well. However, the Neolaw of Entropy has not been formulated mathematically as yet. (9/27/08)

The Ultimate Scientific Equation

The ultimate scientific equation will be the scientific equation that expresses the Neolaw of Entropy. Mathematically formulating the Neolaw of Entropy is the ideal problem for students of the African Institute for Mathematical Sciences (AIMS) to focus their attention on. Please note that the Second Law of Thermodynamics (Entropy) is not the same as the Neolaw of Entropy, because the Neolaw of Entropy will be derived from the unified theory of entropy, which has not been formulated as yet. Believe it or not! QED! (9/28/08)

The Neolaw of Entropy Will Be Able to Explain Everything

I am inclined to believe that the Neolaw of Entropy will be able to explain everything in nature in a general way, because entropy is implicated in all aspects of nature, including the human mind. (9/28/08)

Doubly Pointless

If living is pointless, then dying is doubly pointless. In other words, if life is pointless, then death is doubly pointless. To put it another way, if existence is pointless, then nonexistence is doubly pointless. And, if everything is pointless, then nothingness is doubly pointless. Also, if nonzero is pointless, then zero is doubly pointless. Believe it or not! QED! (9/28/08)

Intuition Is About Subconsciously Connecting the Intellectual Dots

Intuition is about subconsciously connecting the intellectual dots in response to a problem posed by the conscious mind, and then generating a conscious intellectual answer to the problem without the conscious mind having any idea how it arrived at the answer (intuition). In other words, intuition is a subconscious form of creativity. (9/29/08)

Blacks Have no Other Choice but to Study Western Philosophy

Even if Western philosophy is racist, blacks have no other choice but to study Western philosophy, because it is foolish to reinvent the philosophical wheel. In any case, blacks believe that they invented the philosophical wheel, so they should embrace Western philosophy, and learn all that they can from it, because knowledge is power, and Western philosophy is where it's at. Believe it or not! QED! (9/29/08)

A Popular Broad-Based Self-Education

I believe that I have proven that a popular broad-based self-education can make one more educated than most PhDs, because it is incredible how educated one can become using only popular media resources. My websites are proof positive that what I say above about popular broad-based self-education is true. Believe it or not! QED! (9/30/08)

Educating the Masses for the Least Amount of Money

There are no concepts in philosophy that cannot be expressed in short simple language that the masses cannot understand, and that is why I believe that philosophy should belong to the masses, because philosophy is the only means of educating the masses to the highest level of understanding and educational mastery for the least amount of money spent on education. After the masses are educated in philosophy, they will have the educational capital that they need to improve their lives, and become more informed and productive members of society. (9/30/08)

Other Races Study Everything

I would like to remind blacks that other races study everything, including shit, so why shouldn't blacks study everything also? I believe that blacks should study everything, including bullshit, because inspiration can originate from any source. Believe it or not! QED! (10/1/08)

Proof that Knowledge Is Infinite

The proof that knowledge is infinite is as follows: The number of uniquely meaningful statements that can be made with language is infinite, but there is an infinite number of different sized infinities, therefore there must be an infinite number of potentially unique contributions to knowledge that can be made by human beings, although most uniquely meaningful statements do not contribute anything to knowledge. Proof positive that knowledge is infinite. Believe it or not! QED! (10/2/08)

Genuine Knowledge Is Analogous to Prime Numbers

Genuine knowledge is analogous to prime numbers, because there is an infinite number of concepts that comprise genuine knowledge, and to discover them all is an unpredictable process that goes on to infinity, and it also gets harder and harder as the search for knowledge gets deeper and deeper in analogy with the search for larger and larger prime numbers, which gets more and more difficult as the prime numbers get larger and larger. Believe it or not! QED! (10/2/08)

A Unified Equation of Prime Numbers

A very important problem in mathematics is the problem of whether or not there is a unified equation of prime numbers, because, if such an equation exists, it would suggest that a unified equation of nature is also possible, because a unified equation of prime numbers is analogous to a unified equation of nature. (10/3/08)

A Unified Equation of Nature

I believe that a unified equation of prime numbers is possible, and if I am correct, then it would suggest that a unified equation of nature is also possible, because a unified equation of prime numbers is analogous to a unified equation of nature. (10/3/08)

A Unified Theory of Jazzons

Scientists will have to come up with a unified theory of jazzons, because all physical particles have jazzons at their cores. Jazzons consists of standing and travelling oscillating photons, which give all physical particles their mass/energy. (10/4/08)

My Websites Are Analogous to an Unexplored Jungle

My websites are analogous to an unexplored jungle for my first time readers, because my websites have the potential to hold all the intellectual secrets of nature in a natural intellectual jungle-like setting. (10/4/08)

On the Frontiers of Science, Technology, and Philosophy

My websites are full of original ideas that are good for PhD and Nobel Prize winning topics, because some of the original ideas that are expressed on my websites are way out there on the frontiers of science, technology, and philosophy. I hope that some university students will make use of my ideas in order to advance their future professional careers. (10/4/08)

The Characteristics of Zero

The Ferreira Fundamental Trinity, which consists of language, logic, and mathematics, is the characteristics of zero (nothingness). In other words, everything in nature consists of either concrete or abstract abstractions, which are the characteristics of zero, and the characteristics of zero are the illusions of zero. (10/4/08)

Taking Ownership of Philosophy

The masses should not wait for the professional philosophers to give them the right and authority to take ownership of philosophy, because the masses are sovereign in democracies. Therefore, in democracies, the masses are free to take ownership of philosophy anytime they so desire. (10/5/08)

Neoliberal Arts Is a Form of Literature

Neoliberal Arts, aka postmodern minimalist philosophy, is a form of literature that encompasses all branches of learning, because it is a bridge discipline that links, interprets, and critiques all branches of learning using the aphorism and the short article. (10/6/08)

Philosophy Is a Form of Phallocentric Literature

Philosophy is a form of phallocentric literature that everyone should engage in, including women and girls, because women and girls have every right to engage in phallocentric literature, since women and girls have phalluses (clitorides). Phallocentric literature is profound literature and it is very much needed in today's gynocentric (shallow) culture. (10/7/08)

Unconscious Minds Have Infinite Entropy

Unconscious minds have infinite entropy, because unconscious minds are unaware of everything. Therefore, before birth and after death, our minds have infinite entropy. Also, there is an infinite number of minds that have infinite entropy at any one moment of time. (10/8/08)

Zero Entropy Has Transcendental Awareness of Everything

There are an infinite number of creations, but most creations do not exist as yet, because most creations have infinite entropy. Human beings are creations unto themselves, because the mind is a creation unto itself. To exist is to have finite but nonzero entropy, while to nonexist is to have either zero or infinite entropy. Zero entropy is not a form of mind, but, instead, zero entropy is a form of spiritual or transcendental awareness. In other words, zero entropy has transcendental awareness of everything, while infinite entropy has transcendental awareness of nothing. (10/8/08)

The True Nature of Entropy Is Being Suppressed

The true nature of entropy is being suppressed from the masses by elitist scientists, because the elitist scientists are aware of the true implications of entropy. In other words, elitists scientists are aware that entropy has to do with everything in nature, including God. (10/9/08)

There Is a Conspiracy Among the Elite Atheists

There is a conspiracy among the elite atheist scientists, mathematicians, and philosophers to suppress anything that indicates that there is a God, and if people were to read my websites, they will see why what I say above is true. (10/9/08)

I Was not a Good Student in School

I was not a good student in school, because of my poor memory, although I am very creative, intellectually speaking. Recently, I learnt that about ten percent of all students have the same memory problem that I have, and I suspect that they are also creative like me. (10/9/08)

Kurt Godel and Alan Turing Are Obsolete

Kurt Godel's incompleteness theorem, and Alan Turing's undecidability concept are obsolete, because panmultiversal panacean computers will be able to tap into zero entropy and solve any mathematical problem in a finite amount of time, due to the fact that zero entropy has perfect order, knowledge, and wisdom. Also, Kurt Godel and Alan Turing knew nothing about classical nor nonclassical quantum computers. And, panmultiversal panacean computers will be based on nonclassical quantum computer architectures. 10/9/08)

The Masses Will Gravitate towards My Websites

Once the masses realize that I have proven scientifically and philosophically that there is a God, the masses will gravitate towards my websites, because my websites have knowledge and wisdom that were only dreamt of by humanity, until now. 10/10/08)

Following My Journey from Atheism to Theism

My readers will discover when they read my websites from my earliest entries to my latest entries that my thinking has evolved from atheism to theism. So, my readers can now use my websites to follow my journey from atheism to theism. 10/10/08)

An Infinite Regress of Zero Entropies Is Possible

There might be an infinite hierarchy of zero entropies (Gods), because we might be able to know everything about our reality by tapping into zero entropy with panmultiversal panacean computers, but our reality could still be in the mind of a desktop nonclassical computer, which would cause an infinite regress of zero entropies (Gods) and panmultiversal panacean computers. However, I do not think that infinite regresses are impossible in nature. Therefore, an infinite regress of zero entropies (Gods) is possible. 10/10/08)

The Fallacy of the Fallacious Argument

Disproving that the logical argument used to defend a hypothesis is based on logical fallacies or false reasoning does not necessarily invalidate the hypothesis, because the hypothesis could still be true. In other words, there is such a fallacy as the fallacy of the fallacious argument. The fallacy of the fallacious argument is the fallacy whereby one argues that because a logical argument used to prove a hypothesis is false, it means that the hypothesis is necessarily false. 10/10/08)

The Fallacy of Scientific Validation

The fallacy of scientific validation is an unexpected fallacy, because science has such utilitarian value, but the accuracy of a scientific theory is no guarantee of its truthfulness in an absolute sense. In other words, the fallacy of scientific validation states that scientific validation does not guarantee that a scientific theory is true, because the scientific theory might be a case of Ptolemaicism. 10/11/08)

Defeating the Second Law of Thermodynamics

I believe that panmultiversal panacean computers will be able to defeat the Second Law of Thermodynamics, because panmultiversal panacean computers will be able to tap into zero entropy and alter the universe in any possible way at will. 10/11/08)

Retrieving the Past

In the not too distant future, it will be possible to retrieve the past electronically by tapping into zero entropy using panmultiversal panacean computers. By retrieving the past, informationally speaking, with panmultiversal panacean computers, it will be possible to resurrect all people who have died in the past, and who will die in the future, using panmultiversal panacean computers. 10/11/08)

Philosophy Should Belong to the Masses
(Part Five)

Western Philosophy Is Where It's At

The world will have to study Western philosophy, if the world wants to get a real education, because Western philosophy is where it's at. The best and easiest way to study Western philosophy is to study my websites, because my writings are concise, to the point, profound, and they also bring clarity to the expression of ideas. (10/11/08)

Jazzons Are Both Point and Nonpoint Particles

Jazzons are point particles, but their effects are not pointlike, because of their standing and travelling oscillations. In other words, jazzons are both point and nonpoint particles, because of the standing and travelling oscillatory nature of the jazzons. (10/11/08)

Oscillatory Point Theory

Oscillatory point theory is analogous to string theory, but instead of vibrating strings, oscillatory point theory consists of oscillatory points oscillating in a higher dimensional space than the three dimensional space of classical physics. The mathematics behind oscillatory point theory will have to be worked out by theoretical physicists, because I am just a philosopher. (10/11/08)

The Conscious Brain Is a Nonclassical Quantum Entanglement Computer

The mind is caused by nonclassical quantum entanglement that occurs at the synapses of brain cells by means of the neurotransmitter chemicals. In other words, the conscious brain is a nonclassical quantum entanglement computer. (10/12/08)

Time Is a Mental Phenomenon

Time is a mental phenomenon that does not exist outside of the mind, because nothing exists outside of the mind, since existence is a characteristic of the mind, and the mind is a characteristic of zero or nothingness. (10/12/08)

Everything that Exist Are Characteristics of the Mind

Everything that exist are characteristics of the mind, because nothing exists outside of the mind, since existence is a characteristic of the mind, and the mind is a characteristic of zero or nothingness. (10/12/08)

Infinity Has Infinite Entropy

Infinity has infinite entropy, while zero has zero entropy. (10/13/08)

Zero and Infinity Are Inseparable

Zero and infinity are inseparable from each other, because they are opposite aspects of the same thing. In other words, zero entropy and infinite entropy are opposite aspects of the same thing. Therefore, zero can be derived from infinity, and vice versa. Also, zero entropy can be derived from infinite entropy, and vice versa. (10/14/08)

The mind is a Characteristic of Both Zero and Infinity

If the mind is a characteristic of zero, then the mind is also a characteristic of infinity, because zero and infinity are inseparable characteristics of each other. In other words, the mind is a characteristic of both zero and infinity. (10/14/08)

Perhaps I Am Wrong

Perhaps I am wrong about zero having zero entropy, and infinity having infinite entropy. Perhaps it is the other way around. Maybe zero has infinite entropy, and infinity has zero entropy. In any event, zero and infinity are opposite aspects of the same thing (God). (10/14/08)

From Now On

From now on, I will state that zero has infinite entropy, while infinity has zero entropy, because I now believe that I have corrected a previous error in my thought. I hope that my students are observing how my thoughts are evolving, because that is also part of my teaching method: namely, teaching students how to be creative by personal examples. (10/15/08)

Zero and Infinity Are Eternal

Zero, which has infinite entropy, nonexists, while infinity, which has zero entropy, exists. Zero and infinity, which are reciprocals of each other, are eternal, because they always were, and always will be. Zero multiplied by infinity gives rise to everything in nature. In other words, everything in nature are illusions of zero multiplied by infinity. (10/15/08)

Jazzon Theory

Jazzon theory is the name that I have given to oscillatory point theory, because jazzons are the oscillatory point particles that give rise to mass/energy, and all the other characteristics of fundamental particles. I believe that jazzons oscillate in a multidimensional Euclidean space. (10/16/08)

Proof that Philosophy Is not Useless Knowledge

Postmodern minimalist philosophy (PMP) has the potential to contribute to any branch of learning, because PMP is a bridge discipline that links, interprets, and critiques all branches of learning using the aphorism and the short article. In other words, people who believe that philosophy is useless knowledge should read my websites, and judge for themselves whether philosophy is useless or not, because my websites are proof positive that philosophy is not useless knowledge. Believe it or not! QED! (10/17/08)

Bringing Philosophy Back from the Dead

In 1972, I told the US military, government scientists, and Congress that I planned to bring philosophy back from the dead someday, because I thought that philosophy was dead, due to the fact that philosophers weren't doing philosophy anymore, because philosophers were contemplating doing philosophy, instead of doing philosophy. With postmodern minimalist philosophy, aka Neoliberal Arts, I believe that I have brought philosophy back from the dead. Believe it or not! Amen and hallelujah! QED! :) (10/17/08)

The Fundamental Particle Zoo

The fundamental particle zoo is caused by the different shapes that the oscillating jazzons trace out in the multidimensional Euclidean space that the jazzons inhabit. The different shapes traced out by the oscillating jazzons represent different types of fundamental particles in the fundamental particle zoo. (10/17/08)

Explaining String Theory

Perhaps the strings in string theory are not really strings, but are the geometrical patterns that are generated by jazzons as the jazzons move on their oscillatory paths in multidimensional space. In other words, string theory can be derived from jazzon theory, because the strings in string theory are not really strings, but are the geometrical patterns generated by jazzons as the jazzons move on their oscillatory paths in multidimensional space. (10/18/08)

It Is Obvious that I Have Now Changed My Mind

In 1972, I told Congress to keep my name out of the media. Well, it is obvious that I have now changed my mind, so I hope that Congress will make my government files public, because I want publicity for my websites. (10/19/08)

Trickle-Up Economics

The US government has tried many economic theories over the years, including trickle-down economics. But, what the US government hasn't tried, and should try is trickle-up economics, which is the exact opposite of trickle-down economics. (10/19/08)

The Emerging Chinese, Indian, and Russian Creditor Cartel

China, India, and Russia have a great opportunity to form a powerful, and influential creditor cartel, if they were to bail out the West from its economic crisis with their huge reserves of Western currencies. By forming a creditor cartel, China, India, and Russia can have great leverage over the West economically, politically, and technologically, which is the rational thing for them to do. So, China, India, and Russia here is your big opportunity to start pulling some of the strings in the West, and the rest of the world as well. (10/20/08)

Causality

Causality is zero and infinity, which are reciprocals of each other. In other words, causality is infinite entropy and zero entropy, which are also reciprocals of each other. Causality gives rise to phenomena in nature when zero multiplies with infinity, or vice versa. (10/20/08)

Philosophical Collage Makers

I call the type of philosophy that most professional philosophers engage in: collage philosophy, because most professional philosophers do philosophy by creating philosophical collages out of other philosophers' works. In other words, most professional philosophers are philosophical collage makers, and not original thinkers, because collage philosophers seldom produce truly original philosophical works, except when the ideas in the philosophical collages belong to the philosophical collage makers themselves. (10/20/08)

Doing Real Philosophy

If philosophers want to learn how to do real philosophy, then they should study my websites, because postmodern minimalist philosophy, aka neoliberal arts, is real philosophy, while in most cases collage philosophy is not real philosophy. I am aware that my philosophy can also be called collage philosophy, but my philosophy is original collage philosophy, therefore my philosophy is real philosophy. Believe it or not! QED! (10/20/08)

Collage Philosophy Is Seldom Real Philosophy

Most professional philosophers are collage philosophers, but collage philosophy is seldom real philosophy, because it seldom adds anything new to philosophy. Real philosophy, like postmodern minimalist philosophy, has to be original, because otherwise philosophy will just be collage philosophy, which seldom adds anything new to philosophy. Collage philosophy is real philosophy only when the ideas in the philosophical collages belong to the philosophical collage makers themselves. (10/21/08)

I Shall not Be Denied

My websites can be used to conquer the world, the universe, and beyond. However, I do not care which ethnic group(s) uses my websites to conquer the world, the universe, and beyond, because all I care about is that the human race survives and prospers in the future. I am rooting for any ethnic group(s) that takes my websites seriously, because I shall not be denied. Believe it or not! QED! (10/21/08)

What Makes One a True Philosopher?

One is not a true philosopher, if one merely rehashes the philosophical ideas of past philosophical masters, because true philosophers have to produce original philosophical ideas of their own to be considered to be true philosophers. Believe it or not! QED! (10/22/08)

What makes One a Truly Educated Person?

What makes one a truly educated person is an education in Western philosophy, and the easiest way to get an education in Western philosophy is to study postmodern minimalist philosophy, aka neoliberal arts. Neoliberal arts will teach students how to think creatively by teaching them how to connect the intellectual dots by personal examples. (10/23/08)

The Neolaw of Entropy Is the Highest Law of God in Nature

The Neolaw of Entropy, which is about the struggle between the Law of Entropy and the Law of Anti-Entropy, is the highest law of God in nature. In other words, the Neolaw of Entropy is the law of nature that governs all other laws in nature. (10/25/08)

Truly Educated People

Truly educated people would accept the truth from any source, even if the source is a chimpanzee that is gesturing in sign language. (10/26/08)

Elitist Scumbags Will not Accept the Truth from Unofficial Sources

Elitist scumbags will not accept the truth from unofficial sources, because elitist scumbags are not truly educated, due to the fact that truly educated people would accept the truth from any source, even if the source is an unofficial source. (10/26/08)

Zero Entropy Multiplied by Infinite Entropy

Zero entropy multiplied by infinite entropy gives rise to everything in nature, because zero entropy represents infinity, while infinite entropy represents zero, and, $0=0/0=X=0/0=0$, is the Ferreira Genesis Equation. (10/27/08)

The True Nature of Time

Time is caused when zero (nothingness) gets multiplied by infinity, or, to put it another way, time results from the multiplication of zero entropy by infinite entropy, or vice versa. (10/27/08)

Infinitropy Is Short for Infinite Entropy

Infinitropy is short for infinite entropy, which is the state of nonexistence or unconsciousness. Infinitropy is the reciprocal or opposite of zerotropy (zero entropy). I now believe that death is a state of infinitropy, and before we are conceived, we are also in a state of infinitropy. (10/28/08)

World Philosophy

World philosophy has to be synonymous with Western philosophy, because Western philosophy is the only nondead-end philosophy in the world. Other philosophies might contain certain truths, but they are all dead-end philosophies. (10/28/08)

Information Control = Mind Control

The most important equation for all social and cultural interactions is: Information control = Mind Control. One cannot be truly free without understanding the above equation, because the above equation is at heart of all important freedoms. (10/28/08)

Freedom of Information = Mind Liberation

Anyone who does not believe in the equation: Freedom of information = Mind liberation, is a fool, because the above equation is true and necessary for a healthy, informed, and liberated mind. (10/28/08)

An Elitist Education Is an Oxymoronic Expression

An elitist education is an oxymoronic expression, because truly educated people would accept the truth from any source, even if the source is a chimpanzee that is gesturing in sign language. (10/29/08)

Perceiving Other Minds Is Possible

I believe that perceiving other minds is possible using panmultiversal panacean computers (PPCs), but that would not disprove solipsism, because we would be perceiving other minds with our own minds, and all that we perceive are the characteristics of our own minds. Therefore, solipsism is still undefeatable, even if we can perceive other minds. (10/29/08)

I Want My Students to Be Nonelitists

I want my students to obtain a true education, and that is why I want them to accept the truth from any source, even if the source is an unofficial source, or a chimpanzee that is gesturing in sign language. In other words, I want my students to be nonelitists, because an elitist education is an oxymoronic expression. Believe it or not! QED! (10/29/08)

Programming the World with Philosophy

If one has philosophical talent, one can program the world with one's own philosophy over the Internet. The Internet is allowing ordinary people like you and me to have our opportunities to influence the whole world with our own philosophies. Please make use of this great opportunity now, because no one knows for sure what tomorrow will bring. Try and program the world for the better, and you might be surprised at how much fun it is. To me, trying to program the world for the better with my philosophical writings is more fun than gambling, sex, or drugs. It should be noted that the lists of courses taken by students each semester at colleges and universities are called programs. Believe it or not! QED! (10/30/08)

Maxwell's Demon(s)

Panmultiversal panacean computers (PPCs) will turn out to be Maxwell's demon(s) for real, because PPCs will help human beings beat the second law of entropy, due to the fact that the neolaw of entropy will make it possible for PPCs to defeat the second law of thermodynamics. (10/30/08)

Information Chain Reactions

In the age of the Internet, if the common man or woman were to develop an important philosophical idea, or any other important idea for that matter, he or she can publish the idea on the Internet and cause good or bad information chain reactions in the world's population as the case might be. (10/30/08)

Universalizing the Comprehensibility of Knowledge

The popularization of technical knowledge by simplifying it is not dumbing down or cheapening of the technical knowledge, but is a means of allowing narrow specialists in different narrow fields of specialization to understand each other, as well as allowing the general public to understand the technical knowledge. In other words, popularizing technical knowledge by simplifying it is a means of universalizing the comprehensibility of knowledge, and not dumbing down or cheapening of technical knowledge as elitist scumbags would have us believe. Believe it or not! QED! (10/30/08)

The Most Effective Type of Economics

The most effective type of economics is trickle-up economics in which consumer spending is subsidized by the government. Trickle-up economics is fairer than trickle-down economics, which is the only type of economics that has been tried so far, because all other types of economics tried so far by the world are really trickle-down economics in one form or another. (10/30/08)

My Motives for Caring About the World

My motives for caring about the world are purely selfish ones, because I want to be resurrected in the future by panmultiversal panacean computers (PPCs), due to the fact that I believe that it will be possible to resurrect the dead in the future when PPCs have the ability to tap into zero entropy, which has perfect order, knowledge, and wisdom. (10/31/08)

Black and Hispanic Studies

Black and Hispanic Studies can benefit very much from neoliberal arts, aka postmodern minimalist philosophy, because neoliberal arts will open up the multiverse of ideas to students of Black and Hispanic Studies. Neoliberal arts will also teach students of Black and Hispanic Studies how to be creative by personal examples. (11/1/08)

Students in the Caribbean

Students in the Caribbean can benefit very much from neoliberal arts, aka postmodern minimalist philosophy, because neoliberal arts will open up the multiverse of ideas to students in the Caribbean. Neoliberal arts will also teach students in the Caribbean how to be creative by personal examples. (11/1/08)

What Religious People Do not Talk About

What religious people do not talk about is the fact that, if God is infinite, then it would mean that there is an infinite number of Gods, because there is an infinite number of different sized infinities. And, if there is an infinite number of Gods, then there might be an infinite number of creations that are governed by separate Gods. (11/1/08)

The God of Our Universe

The God of our universe could be the mind of a desktop nonclassical computer that was created by a mad scientist in another universe, and we could be in the mind of the God in the desktop nonclassical computer that the mad scientist has created. (11/1/08)

People Should Never Stop Dreaming Impossible Dreams

People should never stop dreaming impossible dreams, because there probably are no impossible dreams. So, dream on! (11/1/08)

Index